GRANDMOTHER'S ANIMAL TAILS

by

Sarah Elizabeth Taylor

Taylor, Sarah Elizabeth, *Grandmother's Animal Tails*
Edited by Elisabeth Irene Quinn and Patrick Bondurant Quinn

Text copyright © 2022 by Elisabeth Irene Quinn
Illustrations copyright © by Donna Aktinson
Published by Willow Glen Publications

All rights reserved. This book, or parts thereof, may not be reproduced in any form without permission in written form from the publisher,
Willow Glen Publications,
Oak Hill, Virginia 20171
Except for the use of brief quotations in a book review.

Library of Congress Control Number: 2022909758

ISBN: 978-0-9998090-3-7

To my grandchildren, who love animals.

CONTENTS

Foreword	1

PART I - CAT TAILS

Midge	6
Flossy, the Cat that Loved Birds	8
Penny	11
Penny's Second Life	13
Penny Gives Her Kittens Some Lessons	16
Jerry	18
Tommy & Jack	19
Muff the Fishercat	21
Peter the Clown	23
Peter's Journey	25
Timmy Jinks	27

PART II - DOG TAILS

Shep	32
Fanny	33
Nip	34
Nip's Habits Varied	36

Nip Becomes a Detective	38
Bernie	40
Bruno	42
Jaco	44
Gipsy	46
Jack	49
Jack and the Running-Board	51
Jack Has a Rough Time at the Lake	53
Jack and the Kitten	55
Jack and the Baby Chicken	57
Jack as a Watchdog	58
Pal	60

III. OTHER TAILS

Toby of the North Woods	66
The Black Bears	69
The Porcupine	71
Sheba the Chipmunk	72
Bobby Burns the Pack Rat	74
Postscript	77

FOREWORD

GRANDMOTHER'S ANIMAL TAILS is a collection of true stories about the lives of cats and dogs that my Great-Grandmother, Sarah Elizabeth Taylor, owned and trained. Also included are some other real-life animal stories! The tales are drawn from actual events in the lives of her childhood pets, pets that her children had growing up, and other notable animal encounters. She dedicated the book to her four grandchildren: Seth Hutton "Shorty," Charles William II "Chuck," John William, Jr. "Jack," and Mary Elisabeth "Sissy."

Sarah Elizabeth "Sadie" Taylor spent her childhood in Humbolt, Kansas; Pueblo, Colorado; the city of Lead in the Dakota Territories; and Wichita, Kansas. As an adult she lived in Nebraska with her husband Charles William Taylor and children (Seth, Marie, Hutch, John and Beth). From 1924 until the beginning of World War II, she and her husband spent their summers on Taylor's Island on Lake Vermilion in Minnesota.

In October of 1948, Sadie submitted her manuscript to The Christopher Publishing House in Boston, Massachusetts. The publishing representative informed her that they could not undertake any new work for several months but would consider the possibility of publication in the spring. The last paragraph of the letter read, "we thank you sincerely for the privilege of reading this very interesting manuscript, and hope you may be inclined to leave the questions of publication open until next spring…" Her book was never published. Sadie either decided to refrain from contacting them again, or the publishing company decided not to commit to her book.

We dedicate this book to my mother and Patrick's grandmother, Mary Elisabeth "Sissy" Taylor Kurth, who loved to hear these stories.

Elisabeth Irene "Betsy" Quinn (Sarah Elizabeth's great-granddaughter)
& Patrick Bondurant Quinn (Sarah Elizabeth's great-great-grandson)
Editors

I. CAT TAILS

Dear Children,

You know that cats' tails are generally quite long and perpetually twitching. Now there are all kinds of cats, and so, not surprisingly, there are all kinds of tails to go with them.

To start, a bobcat has no tail at all, except for a tiny stub. The long-haired grand Persian lady possesses a great bushy tail of which she is so proud and vain that she will sit for hours combing it out with her rough tongue. Then, there are the common cats that we all know and see every day, and they are the subjects of most of my stories.

The cat, by nature, is a temperamental animal, but, if properly fed and cared for, can be trained to trust and obey its owner. Cats demand more displays of love and attention than dogs and they instinctively resent the least indication of abuse, generally striking back on the slightest pretext.

Therefore, in training cats, one must treat them as temperamental children of pre-school age, who are yet unable to talk. If so handled, they will, during their lives, repay one many times over through their devotion and uncanny perception.

With much love,
Grandmother Taylor

MIDGE

Cats are reluctant to move from the homes in which they have been raised. After they have lived in a place a few years, moving one to a new home is almost impossible, especially if they are turned loose outside shortly after the move. A dog will go just about anywhere with his master but a cat thinks more of his place of residence than of his people.

Midge was a cat that the Northfield family in Lead, Dakota Territory, raised from a kitten. She lived in the old barn next to my schoolhouse until she was almost twelve years old. She caught mice around the school and foraged for tidbits from the children's lunch boxes so we all loved her. We enjoyed watching her catch the minnows from the brook that flowed in front of the schoolhouse, or sit on the center of the teeter board when we went up and down on the teeter-totter.

When the Northfields moved away we were all blue, for they took Midge with them. Mary Northfield held Midge in her lap as she sat on a pile of bedding in the wagon box. They moved about forty miles away, a two-day journey. How we all missed Midge and talked about her—even the boys!

One day, about three months after the Northfields had moved away, one of the boys went to retrieve some water from the well, but returned running without the pail. He pointed out the window, saying, "Teacher, teacher, Midge is back!" The teacher didn't believe him but decided to get up and look out the window. Sure enough, there was Midge! She was sitting on the same old rock where she used to catch minnows, getting a drink of water. She was so thin and rough looking that we hardly recognized her.

Recess time was near, so the teacher let us all go out to welcome Midge home! Poor old Midge had tramped all the way back to the barn where she was raised. She lived there next to the schoolhouse for several more years until she died.

* * *

Grandmother's wisdom: If you ever try to move a cat, don't let it know where you are going. Let it get used to your new home before you turn it loose outside or it will try to return to its old home even if it is miles away. My mother used to say, "Butter a cat's paws so it will sit long enough to clean them before it begins to look around, and then feed it well and it will stay with you." But never turn a cat loose until it has become acquainted and comfortable with its surroundings.

FLOSSY, THE CAT THAT LOVED BIRDS

Did you ever know a cat that loved birds—not to eat them, but really, truly loved them? Well, I did! Her name was Flossy. Flossy was a Maltese and in the five years of her short life she never harmed a bird. In fact, Flossy saved many birds from other cats.

When I was a schoolgirl, my mother raised canary birds to sell as pets. She kept fifteen to twenty at any given time, but kept two birds as her own pets, named Bernie and Bessie.

One cold winter's night, someone dropped off a tiny little kitten on our doorstep and I begged so hard to keep it that my mother gave in. She expected that, because it was so little, it would soon surely die. But Flossy did not die—I fed her with a spoon until she learned to drink milk by herself.

When the folks were away I took the little birds out of their cages and let them fly about the room. I had a little switch that I would use on Flossy if necessary when she would go toward the birds. First, I scolded her and if that didn't work I touched her slightly with the whip. Soon she became so used to them that they could fly all around her and she learned never to pay the least attention. Next, I took her in my lap and called the birds to me. They knew no fear, so they would light on my knee or hand and eat birdseed or pick at a piece of apple. All the while, Flossy never bothered them. Soon the birds became so bold that they would pick at Flossy's little black nails but she would just draw her paws up under her when the birds got too rough.

Our mockingbird Dick was another special pet of our family. I trained Flossy very carefully about him because Dick could open his cage door himself and walk out of it when we were not near. One day, Dick got out of his cage when the house door was open and flew straight outside. We called and offered him all sorts of tidbits but he did not return to us. Soon we noticed that Flossy and a big yellow cat were stalking Dick and realized that his days might be numbered.

After awhile, we realized that Flossy was really following the yellow cat and trying to chase him away from Dick. When the sun began to set, we placed Dick's cage out on the front porch with the hope that he would come back to it in the dark. Finally, he flew to his drinking cup, but it was covered so he could not get a drink. Then Flossy began to work. At first we thought she was trying to catch Dick but he hopped away. She crept a little nearer and sprang at him. He hopped back. Then she went to the other side and jumped at him.

He watched every move she made and so did we. We saw that she did not try to catch him and wondered what she was trying to do. Finally, Dick stopped right in front of his cage door so Flossy went in front of the door too and then jumped at him. He hopped into the cage and as "quick as a wink" Flossy lay down in the doorway of the cage and began to mew, as much to say, "I have him, now lock the door." We locked it and gave Flossy a good petting.

One evening, we went to church and left Flossy asleep in the front room. We closed the door into the dining room where the birds were kept, for though she was no danger, my mother never fully trusted Flossy with her birds. The big oil lamp was turned down but left burning on the table. When we returned home, we could hear Flossy howling from outside the house. We hurried inside to see what was the matter. As we opened the front door, Flossy ran toward the door to the dining room in a fit. We smelled smoke and hurried to open the door to the dining room. All we could see was thick black smoke and a tiny red spark in the center of the table where the oil lamp stood.

We retrieved a light and opened the windows and doors. When we took the little dead birds out of their cages and laid them on the dining room table, Flossy jumped up on a chair and watched. She reached her head over and rubbed her cheek against the little dead birds, mournfully mewing as though she was crying. My mother took Flossy into her arms in an effort to soothe her. We both cried too, for it was a very sad day. Though our home had not been damaged, we suffered a great loss. Mother had finally been convinced that Flossy loved those birds too, but it was too late.

PENNY

EDITOR'S NOTE: This story depicts a case of animal cruelty. This event took place between 1899-1900. Some people during that time period did not treat animals as humanely as today.

Penny was an alley cat. She was just a little kitten when two brothers named Max and Fritz, found her and her little sister under the feedbox in the barn. Their mother had hidden them there in a nice warm straw bed when she left to find some mice for them to eat.

Once Fritz found them in their bed of straw their whole world was torn upside down, for Fritz and Max were cruel. Fritz grabbed them, put them in a box, and nailed the lid to the box shut. He then hid the box in the woodshed.

The next day Max and Fritz came into the shed with a wire trap and shut the door to the shed behind them. They took out the box with the two kittens—and a terrible thing happened. They emptied the trap into the box and two great big rats dropped down beside the little kittens.

Penny's eyes opened big and wide. She and her sister then began to fight for their lives. The rats were cornered and they fought too. At first Penny was so busy fighting one of the rats that she forgot about her sister. Once she killed the rat she realized her sister had been killed by the second rat. Penny then killed the second rat too. That was Penny's first lesson on rats and one that she never forgot, for she killed every rat she could find after that.

That day happened to be when the boys and their family had to move away. So, when their father called to them, they lifted the box lid off and ran to their father. After the car drove away, Penny crawled out of the box, sick and sore from the many bites the rats had given her.

After a few days, a young man and his new little wife moved into the house where the boys had lived. They saw the little kitten hiding in the barn and tried to coax it out with a saucer of milk but the poor little starved kitten did not know what milk was nor how to drink it. Then they brought a piece of dry bread and she grabbed it and ate it ravenously.

The man said, "she only knows how to eat tenpenny nails." So she was called Tenpenny and later, when she had grown into quite a pet, she was called Penny.

You see, Grandfather and I were the young couple who moved into Fritz and Max's home and Penny became our pet!

PENNY'S SECOND LIFE

Our arrival brought a great change for Penny's life. We were able to finally coax Penny into the house, which was overrun with mice. Penny learned to drink her milk or cream as any normal kitten would. As payment for the kindness, she soon cleared the house of mice. She learned to love me too because I was always kind and thoughtful toward her.

Penny learned to follow me around like a dog and picked up many interesting tricks. When shown a spoon with cream on it, she sat up on her hind legs, clasped her front paws around the spoon and licked the cream out. She often squatted on her hind legs at my knees and put her front paws out, resting her chin on them and closing her eyes as though saying her prayers.

For quite awhile I was bothered by someone rapping on the door and then leaving before I opened it; but I always found Penny waiting for me so I didn't mind so much. Then I pondered this and watched more closely. What do you think I learned?

Penny had a habit of jumping on a window sill outside and looking into the room, then on another window sill, until she discovered which room that I was in. Then, I'd hear a knock on the nearest door. Finally, I caught her! Penny had turned her back to the door and kicked three times, then turned and faced the door to be let inside. Penny was the culprit!

In the summer, Penny would jump on the water shelf in the kitchen and, pressing her paw on the thumb latch, would unhook the screen door, push it a trifle, and exit without bothering anyone.

Once, when I was very ill, Penny grieved so because the nurse would not let her into my room—she acted as if she would die. One day, when the nurse was in the kitchen, she snuck into the bedroom. She was satisfied then because she had found me.

When our first baby Seth was born, we were told that Penny must be kept away. But Penny said, "No" and hid under the baby's blankets at the baby's feet when he would start to cry. Every time Baby Seth fretted, Penny lay down next to his feet. The baby always quieted down because Penny kept his feet warm!

Oh how Penny loved Seth as he grew up! He could pull her tail, or roll her over and over, or put his arm around her neck and carry her around just by her head, as all babies do—but Penny never scratched him.

One day, when Seth was two years old, Penny thought he ought to learn to be more thoughtful; so, after he had chased her from under the stove with a stick, and from the couch and several other places, Penny hopped up into the big arm chair and lay down. Seth started to poke her again, but she grabbed his little finger in her paw and held steady. She didn't scratch or bite, but just held. Seth looked at her in surprise, and then with big tears in his eyes said, "Please, Penny, please, Penny" and she let go. After that she never allowed him to get rough with her, without ever having scratched or bitten him. Penny lived to be an old cat and always, as our other children came along, treated them in the same manner.

At night, Penny stayed in the barn. In the morning, she was always at the kitchen door when I came downstairs. Around Penny would be a circle of dead rats. She looked up into my face and mewed until I said, "Yes, Penny, you are a nice kitty." Then Penny turned away with her tail in the air and walked off as if she owned the whole world. We swept up the rats and put them in the garbage can because Penny never ate them.

When our family left for the summers, we told the milkman to leave milk every day; but after the third day, Penny was not seen again until the day before we came home. Penny always seemed to know the day, so that the neighbors started to say, "The folks will be home tomorrow, the cat has come home—" and we always came home the next day.

How did Penny know?

PENNY GIVES HER KITTENS SOME LESSONS

One summer just before our family headed to summer vacation, Penny had four lovely kittens. One was pure white, one just like herself—an orange tabby with a white stripe on her head and chest—another black and yellow, and the last all yellow. Since the house would be empty all summer, and since all of Penny's other kittens had been killed by the old neighborhood tomcats, we put Penny and her babies in a basket and left them with a friend in another part of town.

Penny stayed with her kittens until they were able to feed themselves, and then disappeared as usual until the evening before we returned home. When we returned home, Penny and three kittens were waiting for us on the porch. How she got them and herself home, we never knew. The white kitten was missing because our friends had kept it in their house, and Penny couldn't retrieve it.

We gave two of the kittens to two friends who loved Penny and had begged for at least one of her kittens, but we kept her son Buff. Buff turned out to be a great disappointment to us all, especially to his mother. Penny scolded and slapped him with her paws, for he was naughty and dirty. He never learned how to be clean so we had to make him stay out in the barn. He snuck into the house whenever he could and Penny watched him all the time if she was around. Penny was very trustworthy. We could leave her anywhere, even if there was food. She never touched it unless it was put in her saucer. But Buff was a thief through and through.

One day, we heard a racket in the dining room, and looking in, we saw Buff on the center of the table, while Penny was growling and walking around the table. Suddenly, Penny jumped up on a chair and then on the table, grabbed Buff by the back of the neck, brought him into the kitchen and gave him the worst whipping a kitten ever received from its mother.

Finally, Penny gave up and chased Buff away from home. While he tried several times to return, Penny always prevented it until he disappeared entirely and we were not sorry.

How Penny taught her kittens to catch mice was remarkable. She would catch a little mouse, bring it in to the kittens and let it run among them. All but Buff would watch it. Penny would take her paw, catch the mouse and toss it first toward one and then another as it would run, until they learned to do the same. Then, one day, we saw her and the kittens watching a rat hole, and in a little while, they had a rat.

Tiger and Malty grew into good mousers just like their mother, but Buff did not. He was lazy. A mouse might run right over his paws and he would not move. So, you see, he was not helpful to others and did not "earn his keep" or contribute to the welfare of himself or others.

JERRY

Jerry's story, I think, would interest all little farm boys and girls. Mrs. Stanglan had given Jerry to my daughter Marie when he was just a tiny blue ball of fur. His mother had been raised with chickens, and so Jerry was quite used to baby chicks running around. When he was about a year old, a friend gave my two oldest sons Seth and Hutch some Bantam chickens. Soon, our hen Roxy had a flock of the cutest little chicks you ever saw.

We kept Roxy and her babies in the cellar at night, but one nice day, we put a little wire pen out in the yard for them. Suddenly, we heard an awful squawking and commotion. Running to see what was the matter, we saw that a great old yellow cat had eaten all but five of the baby chicks. Upon arriving to the cage, we also saw the cat had killed poor little Roxy.

That night, we put the remaining baby chicks in a basket under the stove to keep them warm since they no longer had a mother to lay with them. We went to bed, forgetting about Jerry due to the day's events. The next morning when we got up, we found Jerry in the basket, with the five baby chicks cuddled up to him, all snug and warm. Jerry raised the little chicks until they were grown and it was time for us to move to another town. We gave the chicks away before we left, but brought Jerry to Lincoln, Nebraska with us.

He was a very large and beautiful cat and liked to sit up on the gatepost watching people walk by. One evening he disappeared and we always suspected that someone had stolen him.

TOMMY AND JACK

When we lived out in the country, we had an old tool house where the rats and mice played. We tried to keep cats in the tool house but in the fall the college fraternity boys made their pledges gather up cats of certain colors—and thus we had a hard time keeping our kittens. Late at night we would hear an automobile stop in front of our house and someone call, "Kitty, kitty!" The next day we'd discover our kitten was gone.

We finally gave up employing cats and started setting out poison for the rats. That ended suddenly when, one day, my youngest child, Betty, who was four years old, came running into the house holding a piece of a poisoned cake from which a corner had been bitten off. We called the doctor at once, for we thought she had eaten it. You can be certain that we gathered up every crumb of the poisoned cake we found and destroyed it. When we recovered from our fright we wondered how to get rid of the rats safely.

Our problem was solved one day when we were all out at the pump, watering the stock and discussing our troubles. Just then, up walked the largest cat we had ever seen. He came up from the field and walked as proudly as if he owned the place. Jack, our collie dog, was drinking by the pump. The cat walked right up to Jack and rubbed against his chin and forelegs. Jack backed off in amazement but the cat followed him, rubbing his head against Jack's chest in the friendliest fashion. Jack sniffed at him and backed away again. The cat would not be repulsed and, finally, when he had won us over, Jack accepted him too. We named the cat Tommy. Tommy arrived on a Monday. We noticed that he never wandered over to the street unless accompanied by Jack or one of us. He kept very close to the family and so we had hopes that he might actually stick around. At first we feared that he would bother our baby chicks, but he proved to be a well-trained cat in every way and was also a wonderful mouser.

Jack and Tommy were inseparable. If one of us went out to the field we often saw the two of them trotting side by side. Jack dug out the moles and gophers and Tommy caught them. Or, we'd find Jack sun-bathing with Tommy curled up between his paws. They ate, slept, and lived together except for Saturday nights. On Saturday nights, Tommy slipped away and did not return until Monday morning. Jack seemed to understand this arrangement.

Tommy lived with us for three years until one Monday morning he failed to return. We all looked and looked for him and even Jack seemed anxious about his missing playmate. We finally gave up looking for Tommy and decided that he must have another home where the people were only home on Sundays and perhaps they had finally come home to stay or moved away, taking Tommy with them.

What do you think happened to him?

MUFF THE FISHERCAT

We purchased Muff the kitten for twenty-five cents from the Humane Society. She was part Persian, for her fur was thick and long, but she was not the dainty lady we had hoped for. We eventually gave her away to a farmer. While with us, she lived out in the barn and was a good ratter.

Just before we left for our island in Minnesota for our summer vacation, Muff gave birth to three pretty kittens. Since no one would be home, we put the whole cat family in a box and took them in the car with us. When we arrived at the island, we put the box in the woodshed and turned Muff loose. For the first week, we hardly saw her, except when she slipped in to nurse her kittens. The smell of fish finally lured her from her hiding place and she soon became a veteran fishercat.

Day after day, we saw her lying out on a big rock next to our dock. The water was over two feet deep. In front of the rock, small pike and perch swam around close to the surface of the water. We watched Muff make a quick stroke with her paw, and in the next instant, she'd jump off the rock and scamper into the grass with a small fish in her mouth.

At night, we never caught her in the act of catching fish, but nevertheless, she brought large fish home to her babies along with snowshoe rabbits as big as herself. How she caught the fish and rabbits we never knew, but we found their remains in the shed by her kittens each morning.

When we returned to Lincoln, Nebraska, at summer's end, Muff continued her hunting ways by catching all the songbirds in our yard. We had to give her away along with two of her kittens because of their thievery. Muff's third kitten was Peter, who I will share tales of next.

PETER THE CLOWN

When my youngest child Betty was a schoolgirl, she participated in the school pet show. All the girls and boys brought their pets. Betty had a cat and a dog so she deliberated over which one to take. The dog was really her brother John's, so she thought it would hardly be fair to take him as her pet. So, she decided to bring her kitten, Peter. Peter was so little that Betty didn't know how he would act around so many children. He was one of Muff's babies and a real darling.

Peter had a little clown suit—one side was half black and the other side was half yellow. He also had a yellow and black cap that he wore on his head held by a rubber band under his chin. He had a little yellow and black box with a lid. Peter disliked the cap but tolerated the clown suit. During the show, however, he resigned himself to both and made the best of it, as we all sometimes have to do.

Before the show started, Betty put Peter in his box and shut the lid down. Peter curled up and fell asleep. She had cut holes in the top and sides of the box, so he had plenty of air and was quite content. When the time came for Peter to perform, Betty raised the lid and Peter put his forepaws on the edge of the box and stood up while he blinked his bright eyes. The children clapped their hands and Peter seemed to understand the role he had to play.

Betty lifted a little hoop wrapped with yellow and black ribbon and held it up in front of Peter saying, "Come, Peter." Peter jumped right through the hoop three times and then he turned a somersault. Betty cuddled him in her arms for a moment and petted him. Then she put him on the ground, kneeling beside him saying, "Now, Peter," intending that he would jump over her arm. Peter looked first one way and then the other way but he just sat there. Then, Betty snapped her fingers and said very sternly, "Peter!" Peter then jumped right over her arm and with a twitch in his tail walked over to his box and climbed inside, as much to say, "That's enough!"

When the show was over, the judges tied a blue ribbon around Peter's neck because the children thought he was the nicest pet!

When Peter grew old, he could no longer jump through a hoop, but once in awhile, after a lot of scolding and talking, he would growl, twitch his tail, and jump over Betty's arm. However, he always turned around afterwards and spit at Betty, to indicate he was done.

Betty didn't keep him in practice, so he became fat and lazy from sleeping too much. We often put him in the garden just to watch him saunter up the walkway to within three feet of the garden gate. Near the gate, he would give a spring and fly like a bird as he leapt over our four-foot high fence and land noiselessly on the other side. He became angry whenever he had to do that in his old age.

PETER'S JOURNEY

During the summers our family visited our island home on Lake Vermilion in Minnesota. Betty was always afraid to leave Peter at home alone to be looked after by our neighbor, so he accompanied us in the car.

Old Jack, John's dog, rode on the running—board of the car while Peter lay in a basket on the shelf in the back of the car. A running—board was a step attached along the sides of cars—some were wide enough to serve as a place to sit or even lie down for an adult.

Peter wore a harness and a leash so that Betty could lead him. She let him out to run when we stopped for gas or meals. He disliked riding in the boat across the lake, but when we arrived at the island we turned him loose for we knew he could not get lost there. Peter took four trips to the island without an incident, except that he disappeared each time for two or three days upon our arrival.

On Peter's last trip, he ran away from us and had it not been for Jack's help, we never would have found him. Peter appeared to be wild and did not know who we were. When we returned home, he ran away again, this time for a week. After that experience, we never took Peter to the lake with us.

Old Jack died the next summer on the island and we got a little fox terrier named Pal. Peter and Pal became friends at once and they both walked with us every evening. Sometimes we walked nearly two miles but it made no difference. Peter walked beside Grandfather and Pal walked beside me, or they trotted along just behind us. Peter loved Grandfather most and when he arrived home from work, Peter climbed up on his lap and rubbed his head under Grandfather's chin. He purred and purred and told him in cat language how much he loved Grandfather.

One winter's evening, I opened the door for Peter to go out and he never returned. He was nearly eighteen years old—very old for a cat. We searched and searched for him but we never found him.

TIMMY JINKS

My next cat was rather strange looking; his hind legs were longer than his forelegs, for he was part Siamese. We called him Timmy Jinks or Timmy for short most of the time.

Timmy Jinks was born in Texas but he came north with our daughter Betty. She was a grown woman and working at the time but was coming home to live with us. Timmy rode on the back ledge of the car or down in the backseat with Betty's Cocker Spaniels Dusty and Panda. He never tried to get away during that long trip, for the dogs were his companions and their crates had always been his home. Once he arrived at our home we kept him close in the house, for we were in a crowded part of the city. He proved to be a very clean cat; when he had to go, he would go to the bathroom and use the toilet just like a person!

It always seemed like something was happening to Timmy Jinks that required a trip to the veterinarian. Once, he got into a fight with another cat and lost several teeth which necessitated an operation on his jaw. The vet could not give him an anesthetic, so he lay quietly on the table with Betty petting him. Poor Timmy had to be fed with a dropper for a while, but he got well in time and was soon climbing a four-foot high wire fence and playing with the dogs who loved him.

After we moved out to the edge of the city, Timmy started roaming at night. All was fine until one night, someone shot him. The bullet lodged in his hip and broke the large bone in his leg. The next morning, we could not find him and the dogs went nearly wild. They gathered around a point in the fence and pointed in one direction. So, Betty followed their point, and she found poor Timmy in the long grass, almost dead. She took him to the vet, and he took out pieces of the splintered bone and wired the ends of the bone together. But, he could not remove the bullet. It was so embedded in his hip that it might have killed poor Timmy to take it out.

Timmy became a little stiff in the hip joint, and his hip hurt him when it was cold outside. In spite of that, he was still a good climber. One day, I heard him meowing and the dogs were barking so I went to look for him. Timmy was on top of the roof of our house! I realized that I couldn't do anything to help him so I asked a neighbor boy to get him. Just as the boy came to help, Timmy pranced over to where a limb of a tree reached within four feet of our rooftop and jumped over to it. He caught the branch with his forepaws and then swung his body to bring his hind legs around the limb. He crept off the limb to the trunk of the tree, then, turned and came down the trunk head first.

When Timmy got to the bottom of the tree, the dogs met him and after each had kissed him, they escorted him into the house as if he was a hero! I saw him up there several times after that but the dogs stopped making a fuss over him. They let him take care of himself.

I think the squirrels used to tempt him to do his high climbing, but they were too fast for him and he was never able to catch them. They liked to sit up on the tree limbs and chatter and laugh at him and then lose themselves in a tree hole nearby.

II. DOG TAILS

Dear Children,

You know that dogs' tails come in all shapes and sizes and are oftentimes wagging. Now, there are all kinds of dogs – and so, there are all kinds of tails to go with them. Some tails are short and stubby and others are long and furry.

The dog, by disposition, tends to have a fairly even temperament. Most dogs are loyal, protective and obedient, and are faithful family members.

Dogs are easily trained to perform jobs. They are guardians of their family. When they are well-loved and cared for by their owners, dogs remain devoted pets.

With much love,

Grandmother Taylor

SHEP

My first dog was Shep. He was the offspring of a pair of Highland Scotch shepherd dogs brought to this country directly from Scotland by a family friend.

My mother often told how Shep kept watch over my brother and me when we were babies. He kept us from falling off the high porch or down the steps when we were toddling around. He napped near us, but if we went near the edge of the porch he woke up and came between us and the porch's edge, gently nudging us back to safety and standing there until we were out of harm's way.

One day, as my mother looked on, I played with my kitten Prancy out on the sidewalk in front of our house. Suddenly, there was a yell. As we looked up we saw a team of horses running away. The noise frightened my kitten and she dashed out into the path of the horses galloping down the road. My mother and I held our breath, thinking we would see our kitten killed. Almost immediately, Shep dashed out, grabbed the kitten in his mouth and got out of the horses' way just in time.

Shep brought Prancy to me and walked away as if nothing had happened, all while the men in front of the hotel door cheered for Shep!

FANNY

Fanny was a little black Rat Terrier brought to the Black Hills in the pocket of an old drunken painter in the gold rush days of 1876. She was not much bigger than a pint cup but she sure was a bundle of live wires. She could easily tackle the largest rat you ever saw and to her, mice were playthings. Her black beady eyes saw everything that was going on and her sharp-pointed ears never missed a sound.

With the coming of winter, Fanny grew until she was no longer able to snuggle in Old Mike's pocket, so she traveled at his heels or hid under the sidewalk when Mike spent his time in the saloon. Even through winter days Fanny preferred the fresh air over the warmth of the saloon.

When Old Mike died, Fanny insisted on living with a little girl and her family. One night, the girl's folks were awakened by a racing commotion in the hallway outside of their bedroom. Then came a scratching on the door, and whimpering, followed by a racing down the hall and jumping against other doors.

The folks got up, opened the door and Fanny fell into the room exhausted. The hall was filled with smoke and the stairway was aflame. It was almost too late. They had no way to escape except through the windows. They threw out a mattress and men below held it for the folks to jump onto. Poor little Fanny perished in the fire but saved others in the building.

NIP

Nip was a tiny black-and-white Fox Terrier mix that my father brought home in his pocket when I was five and a half years old. I had been badly hurt in an accident and was bound to my bed, flat on my back, for a long, long time. Papa came to my room and instructed me to put my hand in his pocket. I jerked my hand away quickly, for I initially thought a rat was there, and then, when realizing that could not be, cautiously put my hand back in. A soft, little tongue licked my fingers. I drew the little animal out and found a puppy! I called him Nip.

Nip's mother was the Rat Terrier named Fanny who belonged to an old drunken painter. Her puppies were born under the sidewalk of Papa's store. Nip was really too young to be taken away from his mother but she seemed satisfied that he had found a good home. Several times a day, for several weeks, Fanny slipped into our home to nurse Nip; then, when he was not looking, or asleep, she slipped out again to care for her other puppies under the sidewalk a few blocks away.

When Nip was able to feed himself, Fanny ceased to visit him and never once tried to coax him away with her. As Nip grew up, he became my constant companion and play-fellow, for I had no brothers or sisters. Since he was very small, I played with him as if he were a live doll. I dressed him up in my doll's clothes, put him to sleep in my doll's cradle and rode him around in my doll's buggy.

One day, I put Nip to bed in my doll's nightgown. My mother sent me on an errand to our friend's house and I forgot about Nip. I was in the middle of my errand when, suddenly, something in a long white dress flew through the open window and landed at my feet. Nip had missed me and followed me on my excursion. Finding the doors of our friend's house shut, but one open window, he took that way of reaching me. I took off the long dress, and Nip frisked home in glee beside me.

Another time, we shut Nip in the house and went to church. That day was a children's service, and a group of children about my age were seated on the platform. However, I was seated in the audience. Suddenly, Nip rushed into the church, right up to the pulpit. The minister made a grab for him and the boys in the back of the church tittered. Nip rushed over to the children and sniffed. The minister made for another grab, but by that time, Nip had located me four pews down and sprung from one pew to another until he reached me. By that time, the minister decided that the dog was determined to carry out his plan and resumed the service. Sure enough, Nip, content at last, lay quietly at my feet until church was out.

We later learned that my uncle had visited the house after we had left for church and Nip escaped when my uncle opened the door. The minister commented that Nip really had better manners than some of the boys in the back row, for they kept laughing all evening.

NIP'S HABITS VARIED

Nip's habits varied: some were good and some were rather embarrassing. One winter, Nip became very naughty with a habit which we were never able to break. I had very long, heavy hair, and my mother braided it in two braids and tied them with big ribbons at the ends. The ribbons were usually bright red, or plaids of bright colors.

Nip recognized these ribbons wherever he saw them. If a little girl walked along the street with a similar ribbon, Nip would immediately snatch it off and come running home with it. At first, my mother thought he had found one of mine, for I was always losing them; but soon, the mothers of the other girls began to complain and my mother had to buy many a ribbon to satisfy an angry mother.

On the other hand, Nip had a trick that pleased us—his ability to recognize pigs. Mr. Bender lived on our street and owned pigs that he allowed to run loose all over town. In those days, people let their livestock roam around all day and come home when they were ready. I had a pet hen, and one day, one of Bender's hogs killed my poor hen when she was dusting herself in our backyard.

Nip saw the hog do it and chased him home. After that, whenever Nip found one of Bender's hogs, he chased it all the way until he got it back to Bender's own yard. The hogs began to recognize Nip too. They learned to start for their home at the sound of his bark. They knew that they would have their heels well bitten if they didn't.

When I was thirteen, I was sent to live with my aunt and uncle so I could go to high school. I took Nip with me and when we went for a ride, Nip always came along. What a time we had if he caught sight of a pig! While the horse trotted along, out over the wheels Nip would go, and there was no getting him back until he realized that the pig did not belong to Mr. Bender.

Nip was part Terrier, so his great joy was catching mice and rats. The first rat he ever saw was in a trap. My uncle let it out to give Nip a chance at catching it, but the grip he had on the rat was not quite right—and the rat bit Nip right on the edge of his lip. Nip shook it loose and then pounced on it in a rage. He shook it and shook it, and threw it over his head; then, he whirled it around and caught it again. Finally, when he knew it was dead, Nip went back to the trap to look for another one, but finding none, he headed back for the dead one.

While Nip had been looking in the trap, my uncle threw the dead rat across the fence away in the cornfield. Nip, not finding the rat on his return, ran around in circles for a minute or two and then jumped straight over the fence to where the rat had been thrown. Eventually, my uncle found the rat and buried it. Nip never missed a rat after that and he always kept the barn free of them. He was just as sure in catching cottontail rabbits, but he soon learned that he could not catch jack rabbits because they were too fast.

NIP BECOMES A DETECTIVE

When I was ten years old, my papa made a sled for me that proved to be the fastest on the hill. That sled was the envy of all the boys, and, many times, the bolder ones would snatch the rope out of my hand and coast down the hill. Nip was displeased with their actions and ran after them and often jerked them off the sled. Then, grabbing the sled rope, he would bring the sled back to me.

One night, someone stole my sled off of our front porch. We searched for it for days. My sled was painted gray and had a sharp turned up point on the front of each runner. Papa had cut my name in the braces under the sled where no one would look, but the sled could not be found.

Some two weeks after the sled was stolen, two boys came to the hill with a new sled. Their sled was brown with rounded sled runners so we did not pay any attention to it. Coming up the hill, Nip dashed out in front of the sled and grabbed the rope, which threw the boys off and turned the sled upside down. Before the boys could recover, Nip dragged the sled over to me and I saw my name on the brace. One neighbor boy also recognized my name on the brace and helped me hold onto the sled, while another neighbor boy ran a short distance to my papa's store to get him.

When Papa arrived, he found out that the boys had stolen my sled and that their father had remodeled the front of the runners and painted it brown, thinking that we would not recognize it.

How did Nip know it was my sled?

Nip lived until I went away to college, so I never had another dog until my little boys and girls came along.

BERNIE

When I was in high school in Wichita, Kansas, I knew an elderly nurse named Mrs. Fuller, who lived all alone except for her big St. Bernard dog Bernie and her pet parrot. She resided in a cozy little cottage set way back from the street with a great big yard. The trees and high shrubs obscured the little house so that one could not see it until approaching the front porch. Even then, the porch was also covered with vines all summer long.

Because of her old age, Mrs. Fuller had Bernie do most of her shopping. She would write a note and put it in a basket, and give it to Bernie and tell him to go to the grocery store and the butcher's. Away Bernie would go, with the basket in his mouth, straight to the grocery store; and no one, except for one of the clerks, dared to take the basket. After the clerk read the note and put the items from Mrs. Fuller's list into the basket, he would give it back to Bernie. Bernie would then go to the butcher shop, similarly acquire the meat his owner wanted, and trot back home. Upon his return, Mrs. Fuller rewarded Bernie with a nice bone or a piece of meat and told him that he was a good dog. That satisfied him.

I lived quite a long way from Mrs. Fuller's but attended high school near her house. I always took my lunch to school in a small basket. Whenever Mrs. Fuller saw me she often would say to Bernie, "Bernie, go and get Sadie's basket," and off he would go. As I would step off the street-car, Bernie would be there waiting for me and, "quick as a wink," would run up to me, grab the basket out of my hand and run home. I knew Mrs. Fuller was lonely and wanted me to eat lunch with her.

Mrs. Fuller's parrot, named Pol, was quite a tease and angered Bernie by mimicking Mrs. Fuller calling, "Bernie, Bernie." One day, Pol called Bernie and when he came she laughed at him and said, "You silly dog." Her taunts were more than Bernie could stand; so he grabbed Pol by her lovely tail feathers and pulled them out. Poor Pol, she was so humiliated that she hid in her cage for a week and could not be coaxed to emerge. Bernie was also punished and for a long time neither pet had anything to do with the other, except that Pol squawked whenever Bernie came near her cage.

Bernie always slept on a rug beside Mrs. Fuller's bed. One hot summer's night, a man pried open the window screen beside the bed and started to climb through the window. He had an ugly knife in his hand and might have killed Mrs. Fuller, but Bernie grabbed the man by the throat. The man gave Bernie a nasty cut on his shoulder and then escaped back through the window. Mrs. Fuller was left unharmed.

Friends tried to persuade Mrs. Fuller not to live alone after that, but she said, "No. Bernie will take care of me; I am not afraid."

BRUNO

Bernie's son, Bruno, was an exact counterpart of Bernie in looks but gave his mistress, Mrs. Fuller's daughter, a great deal of grief. Mrs. Fuller's daughter was married to the leading pharmacist of their town; so Bruno became very well known, as he accompanied his mistress everywhere and carried her bundles home for her after shopping.

One day, Bruno came home with a fine basket of fruit; his mistress, Mrs. Taylor (Editor's note: not related to the author Sarah Elizabeth), could not imagine where he got it. A few days later, he brought home a fine ham and gave it to her. Then, a few days later, he brought home a beautiful fur muff; but that day, a very angry woman followed Bruno and claimed the muff. She said that Bruno had taken it right out of her hand. Mrs. Taylor apologized, but the woman accused her of teaching the dog to steal. So, you see, Bruno caused some embarrassing situations for Mrs. Taylor.

The Taylors finally notified the shopkeepers to charge them for anything that Bruno took, for they never knew when Bruno would bring something home. He never ate or destroyed what he stole, but he was a thief and they were unable to break him of his bad habit.

Once, we visited the Taylors, and I had a basket with two kittens in it. Bruno was away when we arrived and Mrs. Taylor asked me what I had in the basket. When I told her, she said, "Oh! We must lock them in the closet or Bruno will swallow them like a pill. He kills every cat in the neighborhood." We hid the kittens until we left the next day—but it was a fact that no cat lived in that neighborhood if Bruno caught sight of it.

I do not know what became of Bruno—last I heard Mrs. Taylor was thinking of sending him away where he would not be such a nuisance.

* * *

Grandmother's wisdom: Dogs, like people, no matter how fine they may be in other ways—if they are thieves—must be placed where they can do no harm in the community. So, Bruno received his just reward for thieving, by being banished from a lovely home and a kind mistress.

JACO

When our children were young, we lived across the street from the school in Lead, South Dakota. Every morning, at ten minutes of nine, we saw young Marybell and her dog Jaco walk down the street. On the first day of school, Marybell's mother accompanied them, with Jaco walking beside Marybell while her little hand rested upon his collar. He always walked on the outside of the walk as a gentleman should. Before they crossed the street, his head turned each way to watch for an auto. When they reached the playground, Jaco stopped. Marybell would then take her hand away, give him a loving pat and kiss him on his forehead, before she skipped off with her playmates.

Even then, Jaco felt that his work was not finished. He stood and watched his little mistress, never once venturing onto the school grounds. When the bell rang and the children trooped into the schoolhouse, Jaco edged a little closer to the door until it closed behind Marybell. With the door closed, Jaco turned, and, with his plumed tail waving, walked calmly home. When the bell rang for dismissal, Jaco appeared again at the corner of the street and stood watchfully waiting until Marybell's little hand slipped under his collar.

Jaco was a huge St. Bernard and was the same age as Marybell. He carried her packages, and romped and played with her in the yard. He was as gentle as a kitten with Marybell but if anyone came too close, he warned them to stay back with a very deep growl. When Marybell was ten, a boy laughed at her as she bid Jaco goodbye. "Bah, I wouldn't kiss a dog," he said. Marybell turned like a flash and slapped him, then ran, with tears in her eyes, toward the schoolhouse. The boy started after her, but Jaco sprang, knocked him down and stood over him until Marybell was inside. Jaco then turned away and marched slowly home. The boy was badly frightened and so were the rest of the children because they knew that Jaco would defend Marybell even with his life.

One day, just as Marybell started to cross the street on her way home from school, a group of high school students came down the street in an auto. The boy driving the car was busy talking to the girl sitting next to him as he drove fast down the street. Marybell was right in the path of the auto but the boy did not see her, and would not have been able to stop in time even if he had wanted to. Jaco immediately jumped in front of Marybell and pushed her out of the path of the car but he was struck and killed. Jaco gave his life to protect Marybell.

GIPSY

Gipsy was a brown Water Spaniel. One day, Grandfather came home leading her on a chain and gave her to our son, Hutch, as a birthday gift. Now, while Gipsy really belonged to Hutch, she seemed to love his sister Marie the most. No one could ever lay a hand on her—even in play, with Gipsy protecting her. If the children wanted to play tag, Gipsy had to be shut inside the house for she would not allow anyone near Marie.

One day, Gipsy went missing and we searched everywhere for her, especially since she was a valuable blooded dog. Grandfather believed she had been stolen, but if she could get loose she would find her way back home. She was gone for over a month and we resigned ourselves to not seeing her again. But one morning, I opened the kitchen door and looked out, and I saw off in the distance an old bedraggled yellow dog crawling along the road. Somehow, that dog looked familiar and on impulse I called, "Gipsy! Gipsy!" Immediately, the dog's head lifted up and her limping feet hastened toward me. It was Gipsy! She had come home with bleeding feet, sun-yellowed fur and a great thick rope around her neck that dragged along her side. She had chewed the rope in two and escaped from her captors. What a joy it was for all of us at her homecoming!

The following Saturday, she came downtown with me and while I was in the grocery store, a little girl looked outside and saw Gipsy. She grabbed her mother's dress and said, "Look, Mama, there's my doggy." Her mother tried to ignore her, but I said to the little girl, "Do you think that is your doggy?"

The little girl answered, "Oh, yes. My papa picked her up by the schoolhouse and brought her home to me, but she chewed the rope and then papa put a chain around her neck and she broke the chain. Then, he put a big thick rope around her but she wouldn't eat. She chewed the rope and ran away." The girl's mother tried to silence her but couldn't; so I said, "But that dog is my little girl's dog and her name is Gipsy."

By that time I was ready to leave the store, and as I went up the street, two men stood on the sidewalk. One man said, "Joe, there's your dog; now's your chance to get her," but Gipsy dodged to the other side of me and kept close to my skirt. We reached home without anyone attempting to take Gipsy, but we had at least learned who the culprit was.

When our son John was born, Gipsy decided that the new baby needed her protection, so she established her position at the side of his bed, or buggy, or wherever he was placed. If anyone came near him, Gipsy crowded between the person and John and pushed them away. If they went to touch him, she growled so they would quickly back away.

Gipsy never growled at our doctor or nurse or at any family member, but no stranger was allowed near. The children often left their toys out in the yard, and sometimes other children tried to pick them up, but when Gipsy was around, they did not dare. Gipsy seemed to know what belonged to us and guarded it.

When we lived in the Black Hills, we were afraid of some kidnappers who had threatened to take the children of one of our friends. Those children visited our house on occasion and spent the morning or afternoon with us and with Gipsy on guard, we knew the children were safe.

Gipsy moved around to several different cities with us, and wherever we went, everyone loved her. Even though she was a good watchdog, she was always gentle with our friends and those who behaved themselves. Gipsy lived many years and proved to be a great pal and playmate for the children. One morning we found her on the landing of the stairs and we could not wake her. We thought it fitting to bury her under the rosebush in our backyard, where she used to play so happily.

JACK

Jack was a very fine Collie. Mr. Rank bought him when he was a puppy for his son Frank, and took him to his beautiful home on the edge of the city. Jack disliked his new home and begged, as well as a dog could, to be taken back to his mother. Mr. Rank thought that Jack would find contentment eventually. Frank tried to play with him, but poor Jack would creep away from him and continue to wallow in his unhappiness.

The people who lived next door had chickens and whenever they got out of their pen, Jack chased them. At first, he did it just to play. He pulled their tail feathers and Frank laughed. But eventually, Jack killed two or three of the chickens, angering the neighbor. Mr. Rank punished Frank and Jack, but to no avail. Whenever Jack saw a chicken, he chased it, usually resulting in its demise.

Finally, Mr. Rank told us that if we wanted Jack, and if Jack liked us, that we could have him. He gave him to our 13-year-old son John, to live with us at our home in Lincoln, Nebraska. We did not know what to expect, for we also had chickens. We had a big red rooster named Terry that fought anything that came along. We thought that Terry might teach Jack how to behave, but we also feared that the hens might get hurt. However, John begged us to keep Jack, so we decided to try him out.

When John went toward Jack, he jumped up and put his paws on John's chest. He wagged his tail and licked his face as John hugged him. Mr. Rank said,

"The dog is yours, John! Take him." When John got into our car, Jack jumped up onto the seat beside John and did not budge until we got home. Jack liked all of us, but his favorite was John. He followed John everywhere.

The next day, John went out to feed the chickens and Jack followed. Earlier, I had put red pepper on the hens' backs and tails. We figured Terry could take care of himself. Jack went for the hens right away and got a mouthful of red pepper. The pepper also got in his eyes, and then Jack got a dose of Terry when he jumped in to defend his wives. Poor Jack—he could not take the abuse. He poked his tail between his legs and ran to hide under the porch. It took John a long time to coax him out. Jack was only nine months old at the time and although it was a hard lesson, he never chased another chicken after that.

JACK AND THE RUNNING-BOARD

When Jack was a year old, we moved out into the country, and Mr. Rank visited us. Jack was so afraid that Mr. Rank would take him away that he stayed close to John. When Mr. Rank tried to pet him, he whimpered and crawled around to the other side of John, and then he ran and hid under the shed. He refused to come out until Mr. Rank had left. This made Mr. Rank feel badly but Collies are like that. They are a one-man dog, and will pick their own masters if you let them.

Shortly after moving to the farm, Jack began to run out into the street and bark at the autos. Once he started, we could not get him to stop. One day, Jack ran too close to an auto and it struck him. We thought he was dead, as he fell over and rolled into the ditch alongside the road. He lay perfectly still, and so we left him until Grandfather came home.

Several hours later, we looked out the window, and who did we see but Jack walking slowly up through the orchard toward our house. The children were so happy that they rushed over to him, but he did not want to be touched. He had learned another very hard lesson. He never chased another auto, but he loved to stand on the running-board of our auto and ride with us wherever we went.

When we drove to Minnesota each summer, we put a baggage carrier together with an old pad on the running-board and Jack would hop on, ready to go! Since cars only had a top speed around 35 miles per hour and often drove slower because of poor roads, Jack could safely ride on the running-board for the whole trip.

We had two cars: a big Lincoln, which we usually drove, as well as a Ford Sedan. One summer, we put the Lincoln in the garage and locked the door, as we had decided to drive the Ford on our trip. We were ready to go but could not find Jack. We called and we called. Finally, we unlocked the garage and looked inside. There was Jack on the running-board of the Lincoln. He had been waiting for us!

JACK HAS A ROUGH TIME AT THE LAKE

Jack loved the lake and the woods and followed our boys everywhere. One day, when we first visited the island, he discovered a porcupine. Jack grabbed it and ended up with his nose and mouth full of sharp quills. The boys had to pull each one out with pinchers and poor Jack was a sick dog for quite some time.

Jack loved to go fishing. He sat quietly at the end of the boat and watched all around. If a rock or sunken log appeared, he barked to warn us; when he saw the line begin to jerk and we began to reel in the fish, he went wild. He watched every move until the fish was landed in the boat. When the fish escaped, his disappointment matched ours.

One time, Jack even jumped into the lake to catch the fish but he quickly learned that was of no use and never tried again. If we left without telling him to watch the house, he followed the boat on land as far as he could and then swam out into the lake after us.

One day, the boys took Jack over to the diving board on the boat and coaxed him out toward the end. They sprang off the board, which simultaneously threw Jack into the lake as well. Jack swam for shore and walked two miles home even though the boys called to him and tried to coax him back to the boat. All evening Jack did not have anything to do with the boys. They had played a mean trick on him and he refused to make up.

Another time, a young girl named Louise, who had never left the big city before, spent the summer with us. She and our daughter Beth were best friends. Beth loved to take her through the woods and show her all the deer and birds. One day, they were returning from a walk when what Louise thought was a black and white cat crossed the path in front of them. Louise cried, "Oh! Look at the pretty kitten!" But Beth yelled, "A SKUNK! Sic 'em, Jack!" Poor Jack grabbed him and then dropped him quickly and ran toward the lake coughing and sneezing. He buried his nose in the mud and rolled in it, but it was no use. For three days, we picnicked elsewhere and left Jack home alone. No one allowed him to come near because he smelled terrible. After that, Jack left all skunks alone.

Beth did not mean to make trouble for Jack but in her fright she forgot what the skunk would do. If she had but stopped and stood quietly for just a few minutes, the skunk would have gone on its way into the woods and she and her friend could have gone on their way too.

Fear can make us do lots of foolish things when there really is nothing to fear. That black and white "kitty" was more afraid of them than they were of him.

JACK AND THE KITTEN

As Jack grew older, he became a very dignified dog and looked down on all the other dogs around. When they tried to fight him, he just brushed them aside as if to say, "Who are you?" He never bothered another dog unless it became too persistent, or meddled with something of ours.

Beth had a little black kitten we called Boots, because he had four white paws yet not another white hair on his body. One day, a friend was visiting and had her little Cocker Spaniel with her. The little dog chased Boots around the yard and across the porch until, finally, he cornered Boots. Jack had been watching the whole affair and just as the Spaniel was about to spring on Boots, Jack jumped, cuffed the spaniel with his paw and uttered a deep "whoof." Jack then grabbed Boots in his mouth and marched in a very regal way back to the porch where he lay down with Boots snuggled up between his paws, as if to say, "Touch him if you dare."

Jack was so dignified that he hardly paid attention to Boots, but if Boots ran out in the street, Jack would bring him back and slap him with his paw, as if to say, "Behave yourself."

Boots was confident that Jack was his friend and if he was naughty, he expected punishment. He also knew that if he was chased by a dog, that he could run to Jack and snuggle up under one of his great big paws for protection.

Poor Boots did not always find Jack when he needed him, and one day, when we were all away, a neighbor's dog got to him. Boots did not survive his injuries. I think he must have relied on Jack too much and never learned to defend himself. Jack was heartbroken.

※ ※ ※

Grandmother's wisdom: We can't always have our friends fight our battles. Sometimes we must learn to fight for ourselves.

JACK AND THE BABY CHICKEN

I had some very fine baby chicks that I had paid a big price for when they were only one day old. I kept them in a little pen along our side yard, away from all the other pens, and I gave them special care. One day, while I was on the back step peeling potatoes for dinner, Jack walked around the house with a baby chick in his mouth. I screamed at him, but he did not drop it until he was right up in front of me. He opened his mouth and the little chick dropped out, unharmed save for some wet feathers.

I picked the chick up and rushed to my pen, expecting to find it all broken apart. But it looked fine, and all of my chicks were accounted for, which left me wondering where the one in my hand was from. Just then, my neighbor came around the house and claimed the lost chick. She had seen Jack run out and pick it up out of the path of an auto and expected that he had killed it.

I had scolded Jack about the chicken, but when I apologized to him he seemed to understand. He watched every move we made and when the neighbor patted him on the head, he wagged his tail and smiled. When I patted him, he wagged his whole body and then darted off to watch the road for more strays.

JACK AS A WATCHDOG

Jack was always diligent to guard our home from "strangers." One Sunday, when we were all away at church, our cousin Clarence had arrived from another state to visit us. He started to come up to the house from the road but Jack growled and would not let him near. Clarence then walked down the road and tried to come up from the back, but Jack walked along the inside of the fence and our cousin could not get nearer that way either.

Clarence made up his mind that he would have to wait until someone came to the door; so he sat down on his grip (that is, a suitcase) by the side of the road. We found him there when we got home, with Jack still on guard. We took our cousin up and introduced him to Jack. We had Jack shake his hand and told him that he was "one of us." From then on, Clarence could come at anytime and Jack always welcomed him!

Other visitors, however, were not so successful in earning Jack's trust. One day, a cousin of Grandfather's came to visit us. We introduced Jack to her, but she would not shake hands with Jack—so he walked off in disgust.

When feeding time came, Jack could not be found and neither could Peter, our daughter Betty's cat. We searched and searched and all the children of the neighborhood helped us look but they could not be found. Cousin Ella stayed for three days and we had given up hope of finding Jack and Peter, but just as she drove away in her car, they both came walking very sedately from around the corner of the house. We never did find out where they had been.

Up at the lake, when anyone visited whom Jack disliked, he would go under the cabin and stay there until they left. But if he thought them untrustworthy, he would stand on the dock and prevent them from landing until we directed him to leave them alone.

Jack was a good watchdog.

Jack lived to be fourteen years old and died while we were at the island. We buried him in a nice sunny spot where he loved to rest. We placed a great stone at his head and Betty took white pebbles and laid them on the grave to spell out "JACK." We all loved Jack for he was always good and kind and faithful.

PAL

Pal was a little black and white Fox Terrier. We bought him for our daughter Betty after Jack died, but he always seemed to favor me, perhaps because I fed and petted him more than anyone else. Pal was always a little jealous of Peter, Betty's cat, because she and Grandfather always gave Peter a lot of attention and Pal sensed it. Peter and Pal, however, were always good friends. When we went for a walk, Pal stayed on one side of me and Peter on the other. We never used a leash—they just followed naturally.

If Pal was in the house and Peter was outside and wanted in, Pal told me by barking and running to the door. One day, a dog chased Peter up a tree and Pal could not get the dog to leave so he came to me and led me to where Peter was. I chased the strange dog away and Peter soon came down. Peter understood what Pal had done and tried to say, "Thank you" by rubbing himself under Pal's chin. Pal licked his face and they both followed me home.

One day, I fell downstairs, and it knocked the breath out of me so much so that, for awhile, I could not speak. Pal ran up to me and whimpered and whined and pulled at my hand for me to get up but I could not move. The doors were all shut, but one window was open about a foot wide. Our neighbor was working in his yard, so Pal ran first to one door and then to another, but soon realized he could not get out to get help. Next, he ran and jumped upon the chair by the window. How he barked and ran from the window back to me over and over again. Our neighbor heard him but could not figure out what was wrong.

Finally, I was able to move a little and although I could not say much, I spoke gently to Pal and he quietly lay down next to me. He licked my hand and whined some. It was not his fault that he could not bring help. Once someone found me and took me to the hospital, I had to stay for nearly two months. When I returned home, Pal was so glad to see me. I was never able to wander very far from him because he considered himself to be my protector.

If I went to the city, he was content to stay at home, but once he heard the car returning, although several blocks away, he began barking to welcome me home. As soon as I was inside the house, he was at my feet. No matter where I went, he was next to me. People used to say to me, "That dog would die if anything happened to you." I noticed that there were certain rooms that Pal would not enter. But when I went into them, he lay down just outside the door, whether open or shut, and wait for me to come out.

Just before I turned in for the evening, we usually went for a little walk. So before bedtime came, Pal went to the door and barked softly, then ran back to me and back to the door again. How glad he was when I put my wraps on to go for our walk. Then, as soon as we returned, he headed right up to his bed for the night because the day was done.

III. OTHER TAILS

Dear Children,

This section highlights stories about other animals I knew or encountered. These animals were not domesticated or tame like family pets. They lived in the wild and were not intended to be pets.

Most wild animals are afraid of humans and will run away when they see or hear us. They consider humans as dangerous and are afraid of us as much as we are of them!

Some wild animals can be trained to a degree but they should remain free. They should be free to come and go and live according to their instinct and nature. They should not be dependent on humans, because dependence on humans ultimately makes them more vulnerable to threats.

With much love,

Grandmother Taylor

TOBY OF THE NORTH WOODS

Jamie and Angus McKinsie were two young brothers who lived in the north woods of Minnesota way off in the thick timber. Their father was a lumberman who cut down big pine trees. His wages were sufficient to put food on the table, but to earn extra spending money, the brothers set traps to catch wild animals.

One day the boys took their guns and Tig, their old shepherd dog, out to "run" their traps to find what was in them. They were near their last trap when Tig stopped, his hair bristling up on his back. The boys stopped too, for there in the middle of the path, flat on her stomach, crouched a great big wildcat, spitting and snarling. The next instant she sprang into the air. Tig jumped too, but the cat was on top.

They fought wildly, rolling over and over, first one and then the other on top, the cat snarling and clawing at Tig's head and throat. Angus tried to club the cat (he did not dare shoot), but they moved so fast he could not get near enough to help Tig. Finally, Tig got the best of the wildcat, and held her by the back of her neck so that Angus was able to finish her off. Tig had broken the wildcat's back, but not without being so badly hurt that he nearly died too. The boys pulled him home on their sled and doctored him up for several weeks. If it had not been for Tig, one of the boys might have been killed. Wildcats are very fierce when defending their young, which was what this cat had done.

After the wildcat died, the boys looked around and found her home in a hollow tree. She had three little kittens whose eyes were just opening. The boys put the kittens in their bag and took them home. Mr. McKinsie wanted to kill the kittens. He told the boys that they could never be tamed, but they looked so cute and helpless. The boys begged so hard that their dad finally let them build a pen for them.

The boys fed them with a medicine dropper until they learned to lap milk. Later, they gave the kittens oatmeal, but never raw meat. There was no visible difference between them and Fluff, their domestic cat, except that their tails were bobbed while Fluff's was long and always twitching.

When the kittens were about a month old, one of them died. The boys named the other two Toby and Sly. Sly was always getting out of the pen and hiding from them, until finally one day she vanished completely. The boys found the opening where she had squeezed through two wires, and they never saw her again.

Toby became very tame and romped and played with the boys, hunting in their pockets for bits of bread and especially cake, of which he was very fond. He grew to be a great big bobcat and was very strong. He ran out into his pen from his little house whenever the boys came to see him, so the boys became a little careless about fastening the door properly.

One day, Jamie was trying to catch a young chicken for his mother to cook for supper. It flew against the unfastened door to the pen. The door swung open, allowing for the chicken to fall inside, and swung shut again. Quick as a flash, Toby caught the chicken and killed it, getting his first taste of warm blood. That was the end of his tameness, for all his wild nature came to life, and the boys did not dare go near him again. He did not eat his old food but snarled and spit whenever anyone approached.

Finally, Angus opened the door of the cage one night and the next morning Toby was gone. He had returned to the wild woods where he was born. At least, I suppose that is where he went, for neither Jamie nor Angus ever saw him again.

BLACK BEARS

On our island in the summertime, we saw many sights that city people never do. Along the path in the woods, an old Reddy Fox might scurry across and lose himself in the thicket. At night, moonlight might reveal the glowing eyes of a lynx in the brush. On rare occasions, one might even see a moose lumbering through the woods! One day Grandfather and Seth cut across the island when they heard a deep woof from a nearby thicket. A great old bear dashed out and ran across the open clearing into the deep timbers. Both Grandfather and Seth were startled, but the bear was even more frightened. Poor old bear, he had been caught in a trap at one time and had half of his paw taken off, so we could always track him by his three footprints and the stump of his fourth leg. He never bothered us so we never bothered him.

Many years later, Grandfather was eating cereal for his breakfast in the cabin kitchen when he saw a big shadow appear in the doorway. A black bear had decided he was hungry and needed his breakfast too! So, Grandfather shouted at the bear while he banged two cooking pots together. The frightened bear ran away into the woods. I guess he decided to find his own breakfast somewhere quieter. Grandfather and I nailed the empty cereal box to the wall as a reminder of our breakfast time visitor!

Another summer, a young bear swam over to our island to find food. He had smelled the fried fish we had for dinner. We buried the leftovers and fishbones away from the cabin. Not long after that, we saw a black streak go past the cabin door. I decided to find out what it was. It didn't take long for me to find a yearling bear digging up the buried fish bones. I was so excited to see the bear that I squealed with joy! My squeal frightened the young bear and he ran off into the shelter of the woods. Later that night, as I hiked down the path through the woods I almost ran right into the bear. He was on his way to eat the meal he had dug up earlier! The bear was never seen after that night and we decided that he had moved to another island where he wouldn't be disturbed.

THE PORCUPINE

One evening, we were sitting in the cabin around the dining room table playing games, when Jack began to growl. We looked up and there was a porcupine who came to call on us. He could not get through our screen door but he was sitting up looking straight at us. We watched to see what he would do. Soon he ambled off so we took the flashlight and followed him. He did not go far but climbed up a tree, and when we turned the light on him we also saw his mate. Mr. Porcupine had been trying to find some supper I think.

A short time after that, Grandfather and I were rowing on the lake and saw something swimming. We moved closer and saw Mr. Porcupine swimming from one island to another. After we overtook him, Grandfather dipped the oar underneath him and lifted him out of the water. He started to climb up the handle of the oar but Grandfather dipped him in the water, causing him to slip down the oar blade. Whenever Grandfather raised the blade up Mr. Porcupine would begin to climb toward the boat. Grandfather dunked him four or five times until he finally learned to sit quietly on the end of the oar. Grandfather started the motor and when we arrived at the island, he put the oar onto the bank of the island and Mr. Porcupine walked off into the woods.

SHEBA THE CHIPMUNK

Outside our cabin in the Northwoods of Minnesota lived a lot of friendly chipmunks. I liked to name and train them. We had "Stubby," "Scrappy," "Skittery," "Baby," "Little Bit," "Chip," "Dale," and "Sheba."

I discovered that chipmunks can be taught to perform many tricks! Many will learn to eat peanuts out of your hand and allow you to stroke their backs. They might run up your pant leg and pull a peanut out of one of your pockets. Those were the easy tricks!

Sheba was a special chipmunk. I trained her to climb the post on the cabin porch and pull peanuts off the bell string. She climbed up about four feet to reach the first peanut in the loop and the bells jingled as she tugged on it to pull out the peanut. She then scurried back down the pole, opened up the shell with her teeth, and ran back to her home under the cabin with her cheeks full. She would quickly return up and down the pole two more times with the bells ringing, until the peanuts were all safely gathered in her den. We all knew that when the bells were silent for too long, that it was time to refill the bell string with peanuts!

Another trick Sheba performed was to take the peanuts off our toy Ferris wheel. The children put a peanut in each seat of the Ferris wheel and Sheba spun the wheel to retrieve the peanuts. This required her to take several trips back and forth from her den since she could only stuff about two peanuts in her cheek pouches at one time.

The best trick that Sheba liked to perform was with our toy sailboat when we put it in the lake along the shoreline. We placed two peanuts on the boat and called for Sheba by scratching a peanut shell on a rock nearby. Sheba scampered up to the floating boat, hopped onto it, put a peanut in her mouth, and then bounded back onto the land. Of course, we steadied the boat when Sheba hopped on so she wouldn't fall into the water. But chipmunks can swim, so even if she had fallen in she would have been fine!

While other chipmunks became our "summertime" pets at the lake, Sheba was always special to us. Every summer, we kept a can of peanuts on the cabin porch. When we first arrived, we let the chipmunks know by calling out to them, "Here Chippy, chippy, chippy" while scratching a peanut on the floor of the porch. They always knew to visit!

BOBBY BURNS THE PACK RAT

Unlike the other stories here that took place in northern Minnesota, this one occurred in the Black Hills of the Dakota Territory now known as South Dakota.

In the early 1880s, lung trouble sent Jack Hemmingway to the Black Hills. Born and reared in an eastern city, he knew nothing of roughing it in a western mining camp. However, the will to live is strong in every breast, and if roughing it would make him well again he would rough it.

He wandered over to the hills around Deadwood and Lead, and, after following several gulches, he spotted a rather scenic spot overlooking a beautiful little mountain creek several miles away from the hurly-burly mining camps. There he built his cabin and "staked off a claim" to give reason for living there. During the 1880's gold rush prospectors would claim land as their own by marking it with stakes. Jack did just enough work to hold his claim, and no one paid any attention to him.

When September came, he stocked his cabin with provisions so he would not have to go to town when the deep snows arrived. For a time, all went well. He had plenty of nice clear water to drink and food, for his purse was not empty. He also had books—especially his Bobby Burns, for he loved the old Scotch bard and read him by the hour over and over again.

Finally, the snow came, cutting Jack off from his fellowman, causing him to long for companionship. As the winter evenings grew longer, Jack had trouble with pack rats carrying off his supplies, especially his precious potatoes. He killed a pair and the depredations stopped for a short while, but they soon resumed.

One evening, Jack had been reading his beloved Bobby Burns. He laid the book down on his shelf, lit his pipe, and stretched himself out on his bunk to dream. Upon hearing a stealthy noise, Jack looked over to see a young, hungry looking little pack rat gnawing at the leather corner of his precious book. His sympathy went out to the pack rat, for he thought, I am like that poor, scrawny pest, just trying to hang on to life. The rat had chosen Bobby Burns as his resting place.

Jack moved slightly to watch the movements of the rat. As it scampered off, Jack got up and placed a piece of hardtack out for bait. Soon the rat returned, grabbed the hardtack and ran off again. For several nights Jack fed the little rodent. Gradually emboldened, it finally sat on the table while being fed. It had grown considerably since its first visit and soon became quite tame. Jack named him Bobby Burns.

One evening, Bobby appeared and as he sat on the book, his usual resting place, he dropped a pebble into Jack's tin-cup. Jack looked up: "Ho, ho, trying to pay for your supper? But I don't like stones in my coffee." Jack emptied his cup in his wash-basin. As the pebble lay in the basin, it caught the gleam from the lamp and Jack, startled, picked it up and examined it, to discover a gold nugget. Jack looked around. Bobby was still there, expecting his food.

Evening after evening, Bobby presented Jack with a pebble and Jack examined his movements to determine where he got them. He noticed he went out through a hole in the floor of the cabin. Finally, Jack pulled up the board and discovered Bobby's burrow. He followed it for he felt Bobby had more pebbles hidden away. Since the ground under the cabin was not yet frozen, digging was easy.

Jack did not have to dig far until he broke into a gold pocket in a rocky fissure. He gathered up the golden nuggets in a flour sack, stored his provisions and covered up the mouth of the pit with the floorboards for fear of prying eyes. He then packed his grips and went to Denver with his gold. Upon his return he continued to work his claim quietly. He took out about ten thousand dollars worth of gold before the pocket gave out. He never found the mother lode, but Bobby and his gold nugget cache, along with the air from the pines, had restored Jack's health and given him a neat little nest egg for the future.

POSTSCRIPT

Dear Children,

You know that humans have no tails at all. We come in all different shapes and sizes and hues, and yet not one of us has any kind of tail like a cat or dog or porcupine! However, we get to share different kinds of "tales." Our tales can do all sorts of things. They can make our cheeks sore from grinning or our eyes fill with tears. They can fill us with excitement or put us to sleep! They can even help us teach one another valuable lessons. I hope the feelings and lessons from my tales about Animal Tails stay with you a very long time, as they stayed with me and my grandchildren. Maybe one day, you can share these "tails" with your own grandchildren!

With much love,

Grandmother Taylor

Can you guess whose tail is whose?

An answer key is in the back of the book on Page 82!

PHOTOS

Grandmother Sarah Elizabeth Taylor in 1939 (age 65)

Grandmother's oldest son, Seth Taylor (age 5) with Penny in 1905

An old illustration of Muff

Grandmother Sarah Elizabeth Taylor when she was 6 years old with her dog Nip

Grandmother's third son John William Taylor with his dog Jack

A painting of Grandmother Sarah Elizabeth's dog Pal painted by her daughter Betty

A black bear visits the island

The porcupine catching a ride on Grandmother & Grandfather's oar blade

Sheba the Chipmunk on the sailboat & another chipmunk fetching peanuts from the toy Ferris wheel

ANSWER KEY:

1. Bobby Burns
2. Black bear
3. Timmy Jenks
4. Nip
5. Jack
6. Porcupine
7. Penny
8. Shep
9. Sheba
10. Bernie
11. Flossy
12. Peter
13. Toby
14. Tommy

The Author: **Sarah Elizabeth Taylor**

Born March 18, 1874 in Humbolt, Kansas, Sarah Elizabeth "Sadie" Taylor attended Vassar College from 1893 to1894, then transferred to the University of Nebraska in 1894 and graduated with a Bachelors of Arts in Education in 1898. Sadie was a prolific writer and published poet. In 1939, she published a book of original poetry called *Hearth Stones*. An essay of hers entitled "Say What You Will" appeared in the Fall 1944 edition of the magazine *Prairie Schooner*. Later, two poems entitled "Smilin' Through" and "There Is No Death" were published in *The Muse of 1945*. Sarah Elizabeth Taylor died in 1962 at the age of 88. Her Great-Granddaughter Elisabeth Irene "Betsy" Quinn published her manuscript *Gold Rush Girl: Pioneer Life in the Black Hills* in 2018.

The Editors: **Betsy and Patrick Quinn**

Betsy is the founder and Chief Editor of Willow Glen Publications. Betsy graduated from James Madison University in 1986 with a Bachelor of Arts in English. She was the primary force that transformed her great-grandmother's rough manuscript into *Gold Rush Girl*. Betsy is also a gifted writer and has written a children's story, *The Elk of Amor*, published in 2021.

Patrick is Betsy's third son. He serves as second editor and copywriter for Willow Glen Publications. Patrick graduated from Christopher Newport University in 2018 with a Bachelor of Arts in Philosophy and Religious Studies, and is pursuing a Masters in Divinity from Reformed Theological Seminary in Washington, D.C.

The Illustrator: **Donna Atkinson**

Donna is the illustrator for this book as well as *The Elk of Amor*. Donna graduated from the Ontario College of Art and Design (OCAD) with honors in Fine Art and spent a year abroad in Florence, Italy where she studied at the British Institute. She has shown her work in both Toronto and Virginia and has work featured in numerous private collections to include The Toronto Star and The Williamsburg Foundation. Her illustrations have been featured in *Saturday Night Magazine, Newsweek, Virginia Commonwealth Magazine, The Virginian Pilot* and *Ledger Star*.

www.ingramcontent.com/pod-product-compliance
Lightning Source LLC
Chambersburg PA
CBHW040751020526
44118CB00042B/2865